J.J'S ADVENTURES "WITH FAMILY & FRIENDS"

© 2023 Priscilla Ayala-Boatman

All rights reserved. No part of this publication may be reproduced, distributed, or transmitted in any form or by any means, including photocopying, recording, or other electronic or mechanical methods, without the prior written permission of the publisher, except in the case of brief quotations embodied in critical reviews and certain other noncommercial uses permitted by copyright law.

ISBN: 979-8-35092-612-5

J.J'S ADVENTURES
"WITH FAMILY AND FRIENDS"

Author & illustrator: Priscilla Ayala-Boatman

Hi! It's me, Jason Jayden Boatman aka
J.J. This is my continuing story.

This is so much fun. I feel more alive than ever before.
Today I've water my heavenly garden with my grandpa's.

Tomorrow is today if you think about it. That's because every second is a little tomorrow and every later; now it's a moment that needs to be done quickly or else the fairy dust will get to it first.

There are beautiful colors everywhere in the heaven skies. I cannot name them all. Green is in every shade that earth doesn't have. Our heavenly Father showed me shades of rainbow colors just like my earth toy ball.

Once again, I'll visit you again daily. I just think of the place and off we go visiting. Before I go for more adventures, I've watered my gardens, skateboard into the highest clouds, and got my fishing gear ready for when my earth family comes home with me.

Then I talk with the angels and sing with Jesus about all the children in the world. Then, after that I play catch with my new friend Carolyn, she reminds me of my big sisters on earth and me of her little brothers. I've also made a good friend with Eli, Josh, Peter, Heather and Tray from my home town Vernon, Texas.

I told them about going to visit our earth family and friends. My grandpa and others came alone with me. We usually go in chores groups as our vibes are much blessed by our heavenly Father.

First stop Carolyn home. We see beautiful flowers and beautiful lights all around. When we got closer they were fireflies dancing of joy. As we arrived, Carolyn hug there pet cat that was sleeping up from their stair case.

We see her family in the living room reading a story book together. As she hugs everyone near we all dance around sending our loving energy. I know they felt our love. My friend stayed as we adventures to our next stop for the day.

We flew so high and so fast that grandpa by pass us all.
My grandpa's very fast in flying in the clouds and the wind.

We visited next my family from Wisconsin. All my family we're having a cookout. My Uncle Adrian and Aunt Annette family were all there even second cousins. Grandpa, hug everyone and so did I so tightly. We knew they all felt us my youngest cousin Sophia smile so big. I believe she could see us! She waved, Hello.

I'm so happy we visited on time for this cookout. Oh' boy it smells so good. We send out all our loving energy. And they knew we were there visiting them. Yes, we smell still because we are still living but differently.

We handed out our hearts of energy to all could feel heavenly love. Before we took off for more adventures a few stayed behind. Off, to Texas we go!

We stop by my earth home in Vernon, Texas. All my toys and trampoline were still at the same spot. I stop by each room and my sisters were playing games. So, I've join them as grandpa went flying to the front porch to hang out with my mom; she was drinking her coffee as she glazed watching the birds that were hanging around the trees.

I flew around to find my Dad. He was watering flowers outside. Then Dad climbs a ladder and started cleaning the gutters. They sometimes get leafs, dirt and mush in them. I kick some leafs out of the gutters to get my Dads attention. It worked! My Dad laugh of joy and said, "big boy is that you?!"

I follow dad back inside but before passing by Mom and Grandpa at the front porch. I told grandpa watch this, I've made all the windmills move very fast when I flew around them.

That moment my Mom said, "WOW"! And she looks right at me with a big, teary eye and smiled. She then said, J.J. I love and miss you and I know for sure you are always with us.

I gave my Mom all the hearts in the universe as she game me all of hers. All the cosmic system of matter and energy within one being, that's eternal love God gifted us. Was given and received.

We all went inside the house and I flew around so fast that all our earth pet cats were playing with me and got hysterical with excitement as they race catching all the rainbow vibes.

My family later when to church called, Templo Fuente De Vida aka Source Of Life Church.
We love tagging alone with them.

They played music and clap but grandpa and
I prefer dancing with the heavenly vibes.
We usually tag along with them to church.

Heading back to my home world house, Sabrina
my sister saw me and said, "Hi J.J." Oh' oh Laggy!
You could see me? My sister could see me!

My sister has told me about her visit in her dreams.
She visited a school that looks like my earth school.
Sabrina surprised me because that's how it looks like
in heaven. I believe she did visit me. Sabrina went
on telling me about how she saw us playing at the
top of the castle slide. I saw her from a distance but
she was inside a car as my Mom was driving it.

She mentions that she saw my three friends. One having blond hair with green eyes. They all were about my age which is nine years old on earth years. I was so happy and fully of life.

She said, I did the ESL hand sign of "I love you".
We danced and next we flew off in speeding vibes
with the doves. They were big and pure white.

We stop and visit my Grandma's house Elmo. I've barge in her house and yelled, "HELLO ELMO!" All her pet cats jump up and ran to hide everywhere. It was so funny. Grandpa Joe came to visit with us this time and said, "That's was so funny". He saw Elmo and said she looks beautiful and vibrant as always. My grandma was outside feeding lots of cats that don't have any homes. We watch her feed them and she gave them all the care and love none would give in there time of need.

I sang them a song with both grandfathers letting them know God will care for them when there time comes just like he did for us. They meow of joy.

Next, we flew back to the sky with the doves yet again.
How fun this been. This time the group of doves got bigger.

I told grandpa, look over there that's my earth school Central Elementary. We got closer and saw my favorite teacher, Mrs. Boone and my all-time favorite Nurse Mrs. Mandie Thomas.

I flew straight to Mrs. Boone class and there I've seen my Teacher with her new students. I think a few kids could see me. I've waved, "Hello" to them.

Mrs. Boone ask them to whom are they saying hi to over there. They all answered to Mrs. Boone and said, to our new friend J.J. I gave them all my golden to colored hearts and Mrs. Boone a very big bright red one.

Next, I told Mrs. Boone, I'll be back once more and visited Mrs. Mandie Thomas next. I rush to her office like I've always done so before and gave her a big bear hug and also a colorful red heart as well.

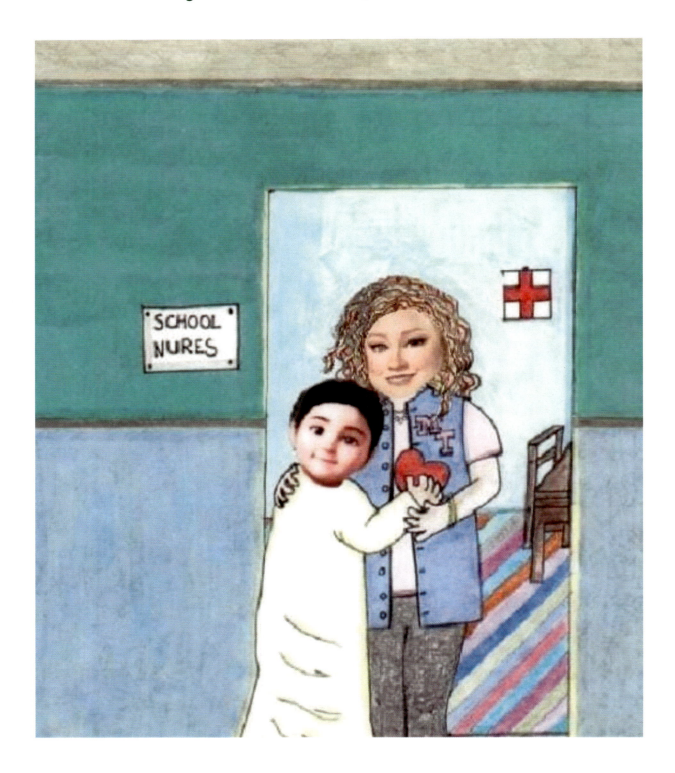

I'm always there visiting. As I've was passing by the hallways, I've spotted a plant they name after me. I felt all there love they send out thought this amazing plant vibes.

We flew high as we left Vernon, Texas once again and into the beyond of outer space.

The world looks like a big colorful blueberry with manmade satellites there's more then 4,500+ active satellites in the orbiting the planet earth that looks like little bugs flying around the globe we saw the planet in a distance.

I told grandpa follow me to the little grey moon that's nearby earth. So, we race to the moon and guess what, I'm faster than speeding Sonic boom. Grandpa said he's a lot like Miles tails from Sonic the cartoon.

Our next stop was the moon. We didn't see Mr. Robotnik there but we saw lots of different size crate holes. Grandpa and I made a snowman using moon dirt and called him Mr. Sandman the incredible space man.

Next, we visit the black matter. So, we dust our self from the moon dust and race to the nearest one. You see there's many.

One, two, three! Off we fly off into the dark space this time grandpa won. Reason was because I've kept glazing at the beautiful galaxies all over the space. It took us a few seconds, we arrived.

The massive black matter is so big and great noting is inside it. There were sparkles all around it from distance burning stars which are also called supernovas on earth.

Next, we left behind golden hearts. We left behind yellow, silver and pure white to bright golden too. So, that amazing place has our heavenly love spread all across the supernovas.

I've told my grandpa, I'll race you back to planet earth. As we took off; one, two, three, I win! We reach back yet again to earth.

Grandpa pointed to the Rocky Mountains. So, off we went into the ozone layer by passing the floating crystals that's in the sky that create our fluffy white clouds and to the great Rocky Mountains in Colorado.

In matter of seconds, we reach to the top of the highest mountains. The sign says, "Mount Elbert". We rested on top looking at our heavenly Lord creation painted skies. We left behind our golden hearts and hung our flags that says; "J.J. and Grandpa Armando were here".

Grandpa said lets visit family while we are here. We visited; Greeley, Eaton and Denver. We saw many family and friends as we left behind golden hearts everywhere.

Off we go again. Like mighty force into the air as we visit and for more adventures.

We flew with the doves and into the great state Oklahoma and we visit my step grandpa David's family. We dance and we scatter our golden colorful hearts. David looks very happy as we believe our present was felt.

Oh' oh Laggy, there was a little boy that saw us. He said, "Hello J.J." as he waved so gracefully. The little boy giggled and said we read your story book that your Mom has written about you.

But, how can some children see me I've wonder. Just like Sophia, my sisters and the students in my teacher's classroom. I think young children can see spirits because there pure innocent souls. There veil is see though. Even on some adults they could see us.

Everyone started dancing with the music that playing in the radio. With lots of love! My grandpa's where all there. So, much fun!

Next, we flew out of there in speeding sonic force to visit next the tallest mountains in the world. "Mount Everest's" that's at the Himalayan Mountains on the border between Nepal and China. There was snow everywhere we look. I left behind a flag with my name on it that said, "J.J. was here!" To whom ever try to challenge my climb, they could put there's next to mine.

I saw my grandpa on the other side of the mountains placing his flag too. We wave at each other. Then, out of nowhere I saw grandpa leaving like a jet into the sky. So, I've followed him to outer space.

Our next adventures we flew off like rockets into the colorful dark space passing by galaxies, small and big planets shape in different forms.

We even pass by a see though planet glowing green with purple clouds all around it.

Out in the distance we see a lonely planet. I told grandpa; look there it's all by itself away from other galaxies. So, we flew right into the center. It looks a lot like earth but, with its clouds in different colors there was no white in them.

The colors there look a lot like heavens but minus the white. There leafs were very big like Jurassic era on earth. It felt like we just shrunk into tiny ants. There trees were tall and all had big flowers. There petals were so soft and fluffy like dandelions. Guess what, there one of my favorite flowers.

Out in the middle of the tall green grass there we're many mushrooms. One catches our attention. It was a very large orange mushroom with white pokier dots. It stood out because there wasn't any white colors on this planet. We walk right on it and felt like my trampoline on earth.

We jump so high and release all our golden hearts into this odd planet. Suddenly, a flock of fuzzy colorful balls pass us like a hail storm or a tumble weed stampede. Some were in bright colors; yellow, blue, orange, green, even pink and purple to gold.

I didn't want to leave this alien world. But, we have many adventures yet to explore. Off, into the unknown sky we went into the space of beyond.

I told that world, we'll be back soon to explore. I told grandpa ready set go!

We race back to our home world as we pass by more galaxies, planets and many dark matters. You see, there's numerous flowing around this outer space.

Out in the distance we spotted our planet earth. And guess what heaven is very near from that blueberry globe.

We wave hello to our family and friends in the heaven as we by pass and before entering earth once more.

As we got closer to earth we see lots of blue water.
I told grandpa lets visit the almighty ocean.

We swam right into the sea shore,
oceanic, ocean going marine salt water.

"This is so much fun!" As we enter the water we saw big colorful jelly fishes, groups of sea turtles, sea horses. As we swam deeper there we saw colorful corals reefs. As we spotted star fishes dancing nearby.

We saw groups of fishes, tuna, sailfish, tarpon, shrimp and even rooster fishes swimming so fast like school buses. We tried to catch up with them so we spin around in a rotating swimming motion creating lots of bubbles. We release our golden hearts into the sea.

Suddenly, a really big blue whale which is the biggest marine mammal swam right next to us and more of his friends gather for a big swim.

We got on top holding on to his slippery blubber skin. Out of the ocean water his large body makes way up into the sky and back into the water surface. Mr. whale, submerge back into the blue marine ocean.

As it leaped out again once more we continue to leave behind our golden hearts into the sea waters. We told them sea creatures this was so much fun.

As we jump off the blue whale and flew faster within the white fluffy clouds for our next adventures. We spin around, sparking golden to colorful hearts everywhere.

Next stop Lubbock, Texas. We visit my Aunt Roxy and family. Sending out lots of golden hearts with the loving vibes. There pet cats kept playing with the golden hearts. They are silly and funny just like me.

We stay for supper oh' boy it smells so good.
My cousins we're smiling at me. As if they could see me.
Oh oh Laggy, they can! We dance around and
I've told them we'll be back soon yet again.

Off, into the beautiful sky we when as we drizzled hearts everywhere. There were lots of doves flying into the beautiful sky and had rainbow clouds all around them.

They all look very magical as we could hear music from angels singing in the sweet melody and doves chirping with the tone. They guide us to San Antonio, Texas.

We thank them before we parted ways. There we see from above the city of San Antonio. Grandpa said there's the house your grandma Gloria and Uncle Gabriel are living at, right there.

And one, two, three we race once more this time it was a tie. As soon as we enter the house grandpa gave my beautiful Grandma a big bear hug. I knew she felt us visiting. She smile so big and laugh of joy.

Uncle Gabriel and his kids we're dancing to the VR game as I've join in with them. We dance around sending out our golden hearts. You see the love was endless.

My cousin said, "Hello J.J!" Oh oh Laggy they could see me! Grandpa said, so concerned can you please tell them I said hi and that I'm always with them.

They responded back, but grandpa we could see and hear you. That's when Grandpa Armando said, Oh' oh Laggy! It was so funny.

My amazing grandpa that has been my guide though this travel said he'll stay a little longer with them and will meet me back in heaven's home.

I told him, Okay see you soon again. As I jet out into the sky leaving behind golden to colorful hearts sparkling everywhere. I've met up with the doves yet again.

This time I've also met up with loving souls young and old. Young once like me age nine years old and others that were two years and some a few months old. And even, thirtieth to ninety years old.

There was one that lived on earth being one hundred thirty years old. But, Oh' boy she few faster than me. I've met up with Krystal, Olga, Royce, Heather, Carolyn, Tray, Eli, Peter and Josh yet again but this time my amazing beautiful grandmother Gloria also join us in our awesome adventures.

We all had a loving white glow and that's God blessing. He was pouring on us all like rain drops. All the love that continues to send out upon us is beyond any loving feeling, it's eternal. Our heavenly Father keeps us safe with the veil that wrap around our souls.

Which why sometimes it's hard to communicate with our love ones back on earth. I told heavenly Lord that I'll be right back as I've went to visit once more for the day with my earth family and heavenly friends.

Oh' the loving light that surrounded me as I've race to see my family. Circling the house where I once lived in as I left lots of golden to colorful hearts all over my hometown. This is so great! I've gave my parents a big hug and my two beautiful sisters; Electra and Sabrina. They said we knew you were coming back, always.

The veil works well when the innocent soul of a young child is full of pure, most children could see us and understand automatic that there's no fear their journey of our souls.

I played VR once again with my sisters to tennis running side to side. To climbing mountains as we hike. And back to making funny noises and jumping on the trampoline.

I follow my family around the house as if my human body was still there. I've never left and I also went to the store with my Dad and wave to kids as they could see me.

Next, I went to church with my family and we clap the hour away. Then, back to the house as I jump on the trampoline with my sisters once more for the day. I've told my sisters I'll be back yet again.

Before I took off, to the heaven skies I left behind more heavenly hearts. In time these hearts do dissolve when absorb.

So, I'll be back. I gave my family one last bear hug before heading out. One, two, three; I go!

I flew like a jet and wave "hi" to my new friends arriving back to heaven doors, as our veils that our Lord gave us for protection from harm on earth surround us all always.

When I got there, Grandpa was already home watering our heavenly garden. He said, Mijo what took you? I said, just flying around like sonic boom around the blueberry globe. Next time will bring our heavenly flowers and give to all our family and friends. We for sure have more friends going with us in our next adventures.

We all fly like speeding rockets and sparkling heavenly golden to colorful hearts for all to feel our heavenly Father eternal love.

See you all soon, for more adventures!

Remember it's a Never Ending Story!